A Book About Whales

Andrea Antinori

Abrams Books For Young Readers
New York

The man here doesn't know it,
but there is a **humpback whale** just underneath
the boat in which he is sitting quietly.
It seems very interested in his hook.
It would be a problem if the whale swallowed the bait.
Do you think the whale would eat the man?
Of course not! That's not the case at all.
Humpback whales don't eat people!
The problem is that if the whale bit the hook,
the man would fall into the water.
Humpback whales are too heavy to pull up.
Wait a minute, I almost forgot . . .

Do you know what a humpback whale is?
You do? How do you already know?
Oh, of course, that's right. If you opened this book,
you must really love whales!
But I'm sure there are still a lot of things
you don't know.
Calm down, I didn't mean to get you down.
It's just that I'm very chatty and as you read
through these pages, I'll tell you everything I have
learned about **humpback whales** and all the other
kinds of whales.

Acknowledgments

The publisher wishes to thank Dr. J. Michael Williamson, former associate professor at Wheelock College and current director of WhaleNet.org, for his assistance in vetting this project. corrainiStudio would like to thank Stefano Angelini, the manager of the educational services of the Aquarium of Genoa, and Luciano Perondi, Silvana Sola, Lorenzo Bravi, Elisa Dalla Battista, Camilla and Gianfranco Marchioni, Maura Benedetti, and Varinia Verdecchia for their support and contribution to this project.

Cataloging-in-Publication Data has been applied for and may be obtained from the Library of Congress.

ISBN 978-1-4197-3502-8

isiaurbino

Thesis for First-Level Academic Diploma

Un libro sulle balene, 1st edition, Maurizio Corraini srl, 2016. Originally published in 2016.

Text and drawings by Andrea Antinori
Translation by David Kelly

Printed and bound in Italy
10 9 8 7 6 5 4 3 2 1

Abrams Books for Young Readers are available at special discounts when purchased in quantity for premiums and promotions as well as fundraising or educational use. Special editions can also be created to specification. For details, contact specialsales@abramsbooks.com or the address below.

ABRAMS The Art of Books
195 Broadway, New York, NY 10007
abramsbooks.com

Contents

Aren't They Fish?

No, sir.
Whales are **mammals**, just like us. Whales are
part of the cetacean order: mammals that spend
their entire lives underwater. They have blubber,
paddle-shaped fins, and blowholes at the top of
their heads. When we say "whales," this includes
great whales, dolphins, and porpoises. Dolphins
and porpoises were named differently before
scientists realized that they were all, in fact,
whales.

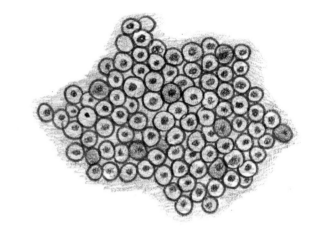

So what does it mean that whales are mammals?
Unlike fish, whales have **mammary glands**
and they nurse their young after **birth**.
Fish, by contrast, lay **eggs**.
When the baby fish are ready to hatch,
they are already able to feed themselves.

Mammals are **warm-blooded** animals,
which means they are able to control
their own body temperature.
Fish are **cold-blooded**,
so their body temperature
varies in relation to the environment
in which they swim.

Not all of them, though!
Some fish, such as tuna, swordfish, and some
shark species, have an independent body
temperature system, just like mammals.

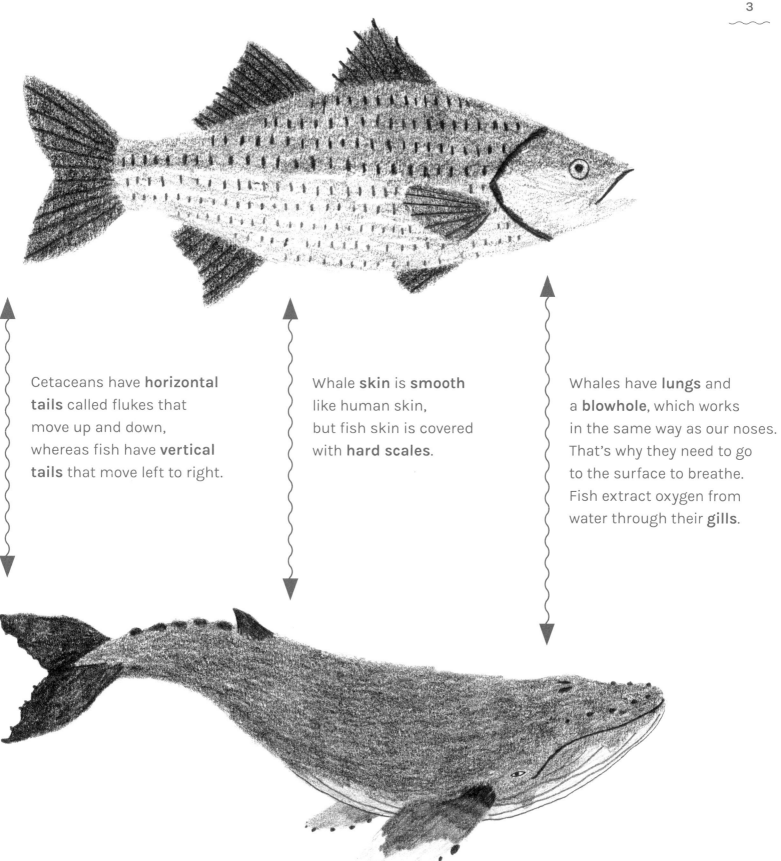

Cetaceans have **horizontal tails** called flukes that move up and down, whereas fish have **vertical tails** that move left to right.

Whale **skin** is **smooth** like human skin, but fish skin is covered with **hard scales**.

Whales have **lungs** and a **blowhole**, which works in the same way as our noses. That's why they need to go to the surface to breathe. Fish extract oxygen from water through their **gills**.

A Good Imitator

Whale Shark
Rhincodon typus
Order: Orectolobiformes
Family: Rhincodontidae

Length: 39–66 ft (12–20 m)
Weight: 39,683–74,957 lb (18–34 T)

There is a shark who wants to look like a whale so much, it has become as large as one! I'm talking about the **whale shark**, the largest fish in the world. Don't get too frightened, though—it is completely harmless to humans. To be like a whale, you have to eat like a whale: Unlike other sharks, whale sharks do not feed on other large animals. Like whales, they prefer to eat tiny crustaceans that are filtered out of the water with their mouths. Don't forget that the whale shark is still a **fish** in all respects: It uses **gills** to breathe and its young hatch from **eggs** inside its body.

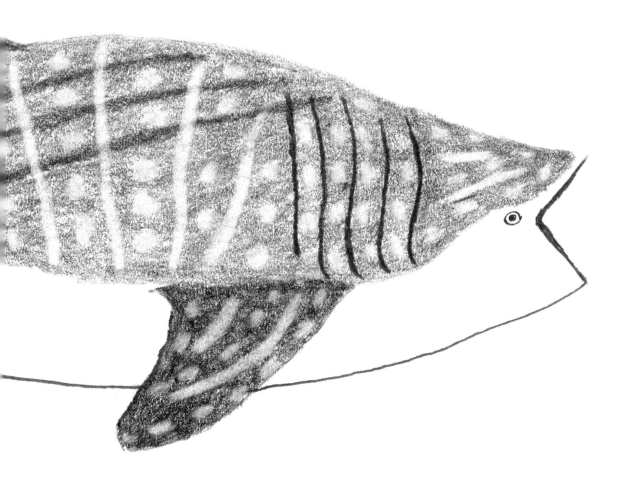

Baleen . . .

Cetaceans are divided into two main groups: **baleen whales** and **toothed whales**.

What are baleen whales?
And what are toothed whales?

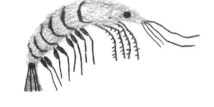

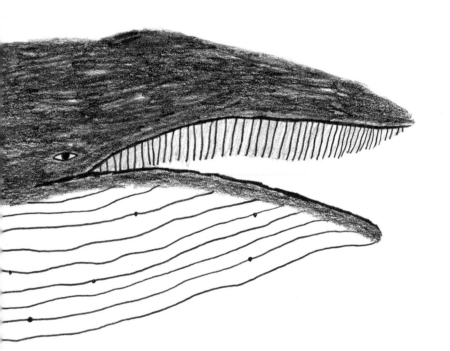

Baleen Whales
Baleen whales are more similar to our idea of a whale because, in the majority of cases, they are larger. They have their name because instead of teeth they have **baleen plates** (the taxonomic name, Mysticeti, means "whale with moustache" in Greek), a long plate that hangs from the top of the mouth.
Baleen whales only eat tiny animals, like **krill** (a type of prawn) or small fish. They don't need teeth to grab or bite them. **Baleen plates** are used to help separate food from seawater. There are about eleven different species of baleen whales, compared to about seventy different types of toothed whales.

Have you noticed that **baleen plates** look like the teeth on a comb?

or Toothed?

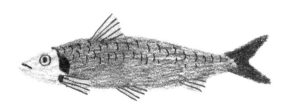

Toothed Whales

Toothed whales are often the smaller centaceans Most of them are closer to dolphins, the most famous members of the group, but others, such as sperm and killer whales, are more easily compared to larger whales.

Have you ever heard the word *odontologist*? I'm talking about the dentist, the tooth doctor. If you think about it, it sounds like the word *Odontoceti*, which is the taxonomic name for toothed whales and means "whale with **teeth**" in Greek. These whales eat larger animals, such as squid or fish of varying size. However, the teeth of these animals are not like our own, which are divided into different shapes suitable for different uses. Toothed whale teeth are all the same pointed shape, like mini harpoons used to seize prey that they swallow whole.

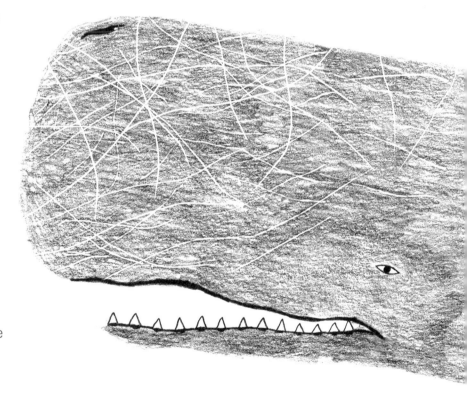

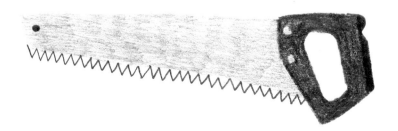

And now looking at a **toothed whale**'s teeth, you can't help but think of a saw!

A Long Time Ago

Whales have not always been marine animals. This is the result of a long process of evolution! At first, they had legs and walked on land like other mammals.

The first **cetacean** that appeared on the face of the earth was the *Pakicetus*, about fifty million years ago.

Indohyus
More than 50 million years ago
Length: 15–28 in (40–70 cm)

Pakicetus
55 million years ago
Length: 39–63 in (100–160 cm)

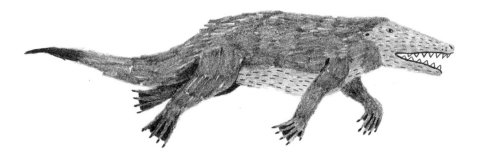

Ambulocetus
50–48 million years ago
Length: 10 ft (3 m)

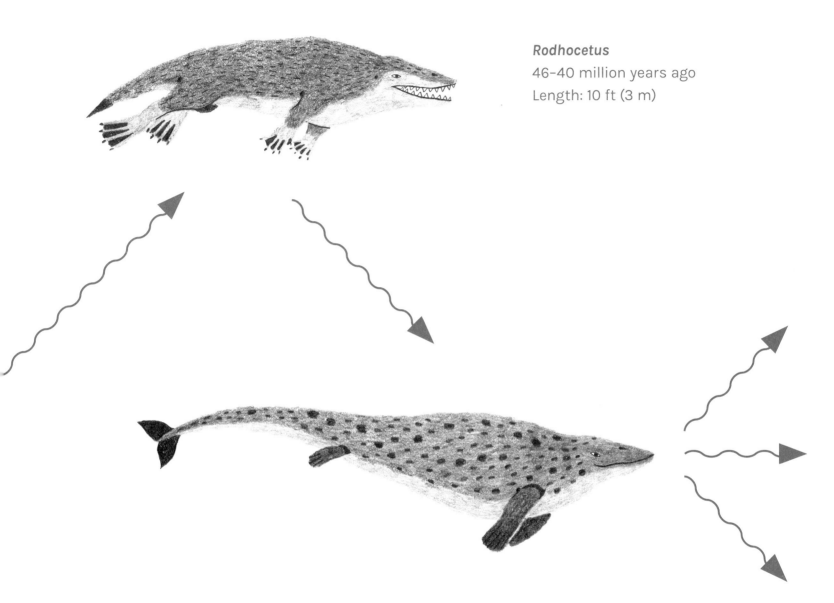

Rodhocetus
46–40 million years ago
Length: 10 ft (3 m)

Dorudon
41–33 million years ago
Length: 16 ft (5 m)

Primitive cetaceans are called **archaeoceti**. They were similar to **ungulates**, mammals such as camels, cows, horses and, in particular, hippos. The transition from land to water was gradual. Their hind legs gradually narrowed until they disappeared and a tail developed, as did the caudal fin, which is ideal for swimming.

Nowadays

When we talk about **whales**, we often mean
large cetaceans, but there are much fewer
large whales than we imagine. Let me explain.
Baleen whales are divided into **three families**:

The Right Whale Family
Balaenidae
(Bowhead whales)

The Rorqual Family
Balaenopteridae
(Fin whales)

The Eschrichtiidae Family
Eschrichtiidae
(Gray whales)

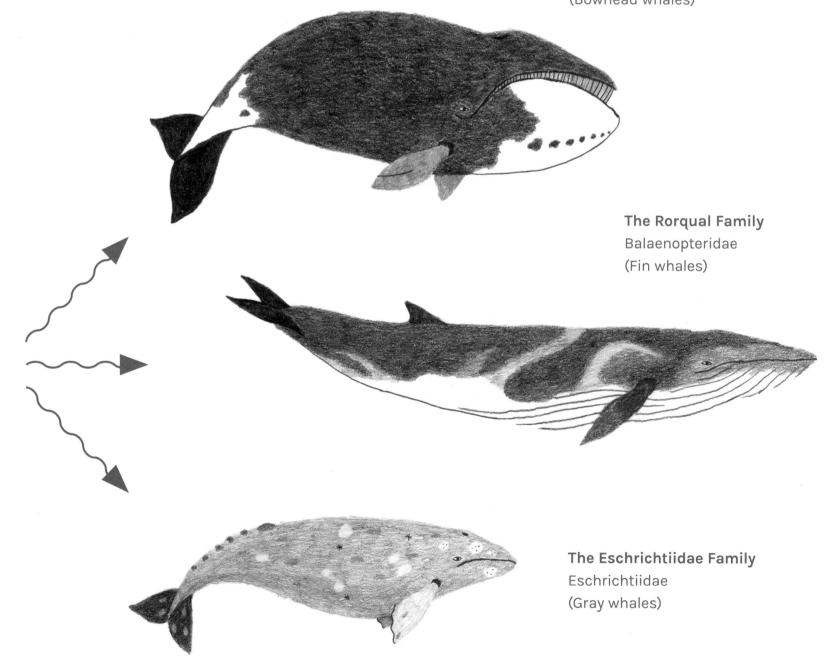

Right whales, or *Balaenidae,*
are the hardiest of all cetaceans,
and they are never in a hurry.
They are always swimming along
slowly and peacefully.
They can be recognized by their heads:
The head is enormous, with a typical arch shape.
It is so big that it can sometimes make up
almost one third of the whale's entire body.
Their **baleen plates** are particularly long,
measuring up to 13 feet (4 m) in length.

Rorqual whales, like fin whales for example,
have two qualities that make them unique
among baleen whales: To start with, they have
fins on their backs, the **dorsal fin**.
As if that were not enough, they also have
ventral pleats (folds on the throat) on their
undersides that allow them to increase the
size of their mouths and take in as much
food as they can. Their long, slender bodies
are particularly hydrodynamic, ideal for
swimming at full speed. They are also called
Balaenopteridae.

The **Eschrichtiidae** family is very strange
indeed. It is made up of only one member,
the **gray whale**. If you look at it carefully,
it seems to be a mixture of a right whale and
a rorqual. It has a **hump** that looks like the
rorquals' dorsal fins, as well as some small
folds of skin.
It has the typical **curved profile** of the whale,
even if it is somewhat less pronounced.
Their bodies are also halfway between the other
two families: The gray whale is thinner than
a right whale but more robust than a rorqual.

Who Is Biggest?

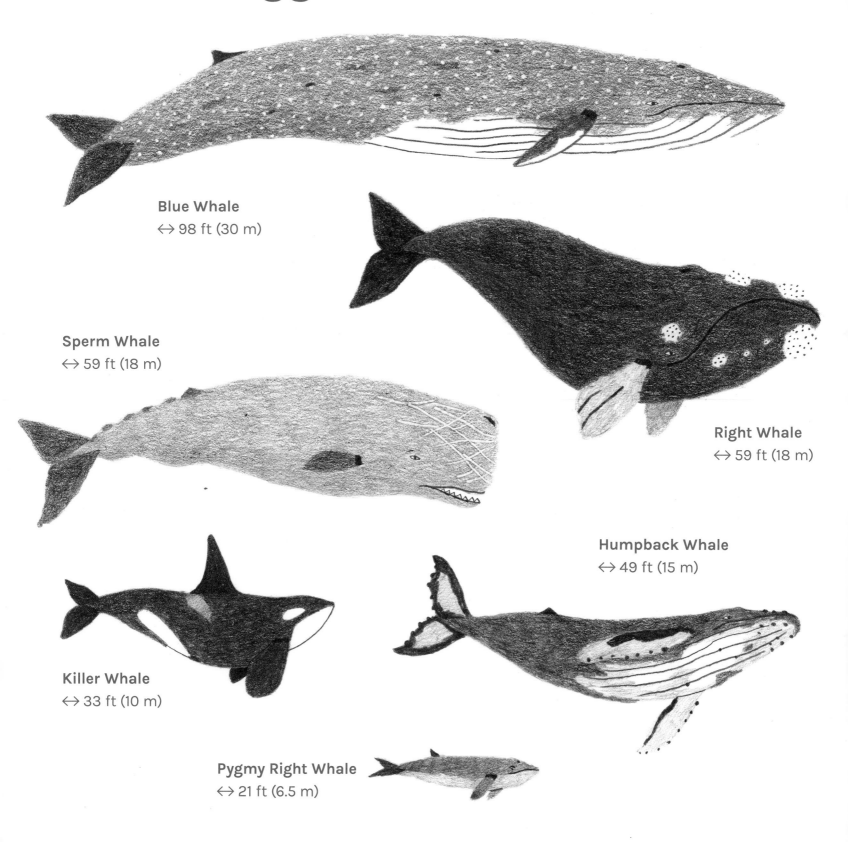

Blue Whale
↔ 98 ft (30 m)

Sperm Whale
↔ 59 ft (18 m)

Right Whale
↔ 59 ft (18 m)

Humpback Whale
↔ 49 ft (15 m)

Killer Whale
↔ 33 ft (10 m)

Pygmy Right Whale
↔ 21 ft (6.5 m)

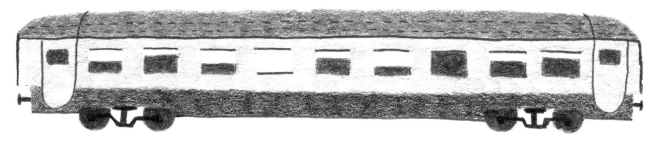

Train Carriage
↔ 85 ft (26 m)

Beech-Tree
↕ 49 ft (15 m)

Hot-Air Balloon
↕ 66 ft (20 m)
↔ 59 ft (18 m)

Tyrannosaurus Rex
↕ 26 ft (8 m)
↔ 43 ft (13 m)

African Elephant
↔ 21 ft (6.5 m)

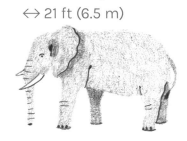

Human
↕ 5.5 ft (1.70 m)

Water in the Mouth

Whales get the water they need to survive from the food they eat. Just like other mammals, they don't want to drink lots of salty seawater. When whales eat, they need to make sure that they don't drink any. That's not easy when you live in the sea! Luckily, they have baleen plates, which they use to solve this problem.

The first step is getting both **food** and **seawater** into their mouths. Each whale has its own way of doing this. **Right whales** swim very **slowly,** close to the surface of the water. When the right whales are eating, they swim through the water constantly filtering out the food, usually copepods, and then periodically close their mouths to swallow the plankton they captured. **Rorqual whales,** on the other hand, are much **quicker** and they spring on their prey, usually a school or concentration of prey, with an open mouth, taking a lot of seawater in addition to their food into their mouths.

Once everything is in a rorqual's mouth, they need to get the water out without allowing their prey to escape! The dense structure of the **baleen plates** acts as a **filter**: whales push the water out of their mouths **with their tongues**, pushing the water between the baleen plates. Captured krill, fish, or other food are too big to pass through, so they remain trapped inside the mouth. The whale then swallows the captured food whole.

If you think about it, the plate works similarly to a colander. Both water and food enter, but the food remains after the water is drained away.

A Constant Mouthful

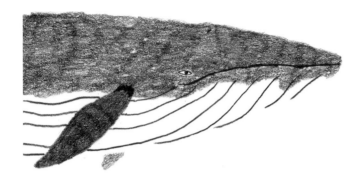

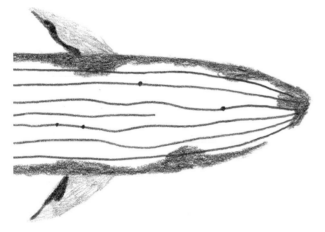

Like the blue whale, underneath rorquals you see nothing but **folds of skin**, from the mouth to the belly. These special folds or ventral pleats help the mouth transform into an extraordinarily spacious hollow. An adult blue whale can hold up to 198,416 pounds (90 T) of water and fish in its mouth. There is no "superpower" greater than this while hunting. Why chase after one fish at a time when you can swallow a whole school in one gulp?

Have you ever seen an accordion? The central bellows on this instrument work by expanding in exactly the same way as the blue whale's belly!

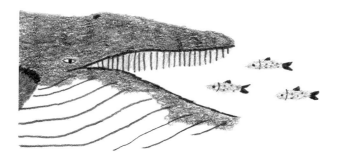

This is just the beginning . . .

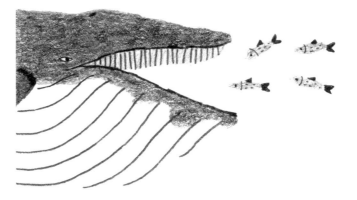

We're not even halfway there!

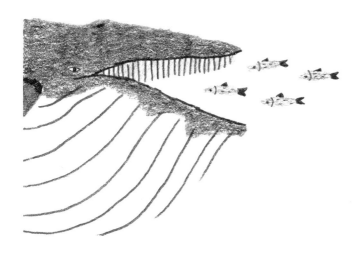

There's still a hole to be filled . . .

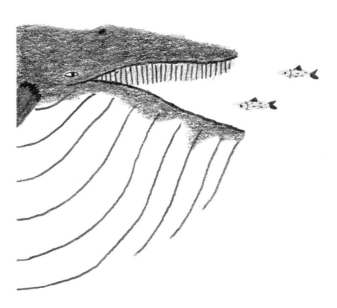

The last two, I promise!

A blue whale can hold food and water weighing up to a third of its entire body weight in its mouth.
So if a blue whale weighs around 396,832 pounds (180 T), it could hold 132,277 pounds (60 T) of water in its mouth!

Enjoy Your Meal

Did a whale eat Pinocchio?!
You're getting confused—that was actually a shark!
Whales don't eat humans *or* marionettes!

Whales don't chew their food—they swallow it
whole. Before reaching the stomach, food
passes through the whale's pharynx which, in larger
whales, is about the size of a small beach ball.
Even the thinnest human wouldn't pass through it!

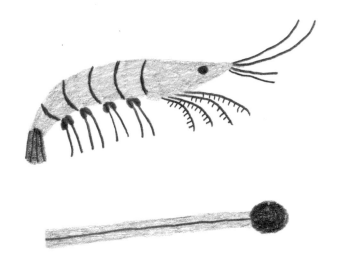

So how do they satisfy their appetites?
If they can't eat big things, the alternative is to
eat lots of small things!
A whale's favorite food is **krill**, a crustacean
that is about as big as a matchstick.
The sea is full of these little creatures, and
blue whales are well aware of this, eating up to
forty million krill each day.

Cetaceans have **three stomachs** where food is digested.

The **first stomach** performs a similar function to our chewing. It is equipped with "teeth," and when it contracts, food is broken down.

In the **second stomach**, which is the main one, there are a number of different glands that release gastric fluids that cause food to dissolve.

Digestion ends in the **third stomach**, where food passes into the intestine and nutrients are absorbed.

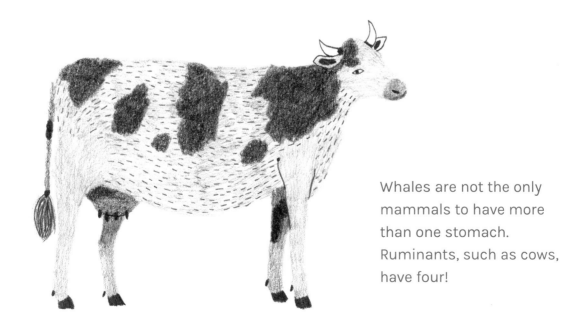

Whales are not the only mammals to have more than one stomach. Ruminants, such as cows, have four!

Upturned Nose

I bet you have been taught how to swim underwater. When you dive down, you normally take a deep breath and hold it until you get back to the surface for more air. Whales do the same thing, only they can hold their breath for much longer. Sperm whales can do it for two hours.

Your nose is in the middle of your face, but a whale's nose, called a **blowhole**, is on top of its head.

Baleen whales have two external blowholes, whereas toothed whales only have one.

When whales come up to breathe, they rise in a vertical arc on the surface of the water. The blowhole opens and they **exhale**, releasing the **blow** that is typical of whales. Then they **breathe in** immediately, gathering up the necessary oxygen to dive down again.

When whales sleep, they remain close to the surface in order to breathe. Some even like to keep their blowholes out of the water while they sleep. Humans breathe involuntarily, but that is not the case with whales. Even when they sleep, they must remain conscious. A whale can do this because it sleeps on only one half of its brain at a time. When one half is rested, it changes sides of the brain.

Watch Out for Splashes

Blue Whale
Thin and straight,
this whale's blow takes
first prize with
a height of 29 feet (9 m).

Bowhead Whale
This V-shaped blow into
reaches 23 feet (7 m).

When a whale emerges from the water to breathe, it looks like a huge jet of water comes out of the blowhole. What really comes out is mostly air, and it is known as the **blow**. It's important to be able to distinguish between the blows of marine mammals! It's also important to distinguish between the blows of different whales. Even for experts, it is difficult to see the whales underwater, so the scientists need to be able to recognize what can be seen above water.

And how can you fail to notice a blow that can reach the height of a three-story building, or even taller? Each whale has its own type of blow, and it can be recognized by its momentum, shape, and power.

But what is blow made from?

It is a mixture of air, water vapor, and droplets of oil and mucus contained within the body of the whale.

Humpback Whale

This blow is different because it is usually wider than it is long. It reaches 10 feet (3 m) in height.

Sperm Whale

The blow of a sperm whale is instantly recognizable. It is projected forward and rises up to 7 feet (2 m).

Oops, this is just a scuba diver's breath!

Born Acrobats

Oh yes, some whales, like the humpback whale, are natural acrobats. They jump, splash, and flip over on themselves.

But what are their best stunts?

Breaching

Make sure you don't miss it because **breaching** is the only way you'll be able to see an entire whale! This is when the whale jumps completely out of the water and falls on its back or belly, twisting around completely.

The cause of this behavior is still unknown. Some scientists say that it is for courtship or challenge among whales. Others think it is a way to get rid of parasites. But it could just be a way for them to play.

Lobtailing

If you see a whale's tail rise up out of the water, be careful: You might be in line for a **slap**! **Lobtailing** is when a whale lifts its tail out of the water and smacks the surface. It is said to be an intimidating gesture or, because of the loud noise it makes, a way of communicating with the rest of the pod.

Spyhopping

"Who goes there?!"
Looking right, looking left: **Spyhopping**
is the name for a whale popping its head out
of the water to see what's going on up there.

Logging

You get tired performing all these tricks!
After a day of leaping, you need to rest
a little, floating on the water, as straight
as a **tree trunk**. **Logging** is generally a group
activity, with all the whales in a pod
relaxing, "stretched out" in the same direction.

Top Qualities

Echolocation

It's not always easy to see where you're going underwater, even when you have a good view. This is why whales, and particularly toothed whales, have developed a sixth sense to help them get around. Toothed whales use sound to communicate, navigate, and echolocate. They manage to "see" thanks to the **echo** caused by every single sound.

This is how cetaceans communicate: The sounds they emit bounce off the closest obstacle and head back toward the whale. It can be hard for us to imagine, but echoes allow whales to orient themselves in the darkest depths and to locate their prey. Do you know how a ship's radar works? Well, this works in exactly the same way.

Language

Like us humans, whales can also "talk" by making sounds that have meanings to other whales. Whales can make a great variety of sounds, and each of them can be associated with a different action or situation. There are even a number of "**dialects**" between members of the same species that change from group to group.

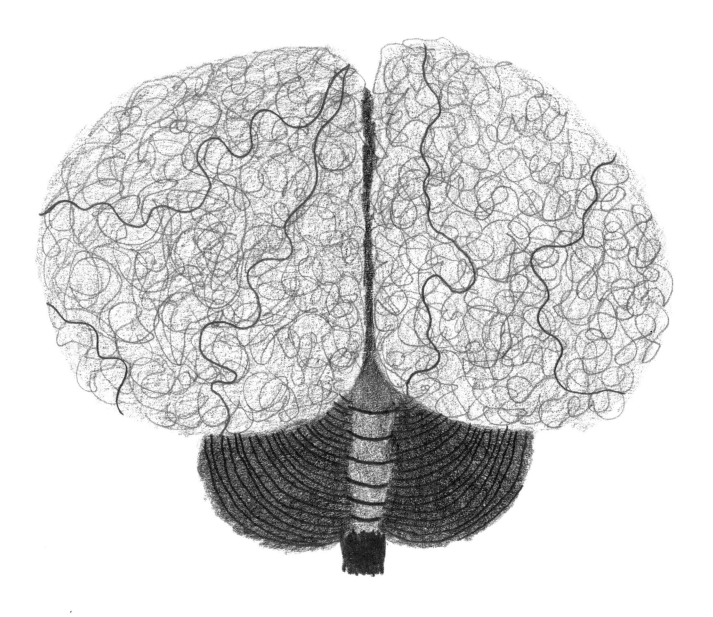

Intelligence

A whale's brain is, in some respects, very similar to a human brain. Is their **intelligence** similar to ours?

Many argue that whales' cleverness is due to the size of their brains, obviously in relation to the immense size of their bodies.

But instead of just looking at the brain, it is important to look at how whales behave.

Much of their behavior is complex enough to be a true test of their intelligence.

They are **quick learners**, and their knowledge is passed down between family members. Some cetaceans also invent their own strategies, especially when hunting and defending members of their pods.

Around the World

Which city do you live in?
If you were to ask this question
to whales, they wouldn't be able to give
you an answer.
They are constantly on the move! They migrate
throughout the entire year, in **winter** and
summer, from the south to the north and
from the north to the south.

Most baleen whales **reproduce** and start
families in winter. It is important that
newborns start their development in warmer
waters: "Let's go! Swim toward the **equator**."

In the warmer seasons, whales travel toward
the poles to **feed.** As the ice melts, there are
greater numbers of krill, fish, and zooplankton,
whales' favorite things to eat.

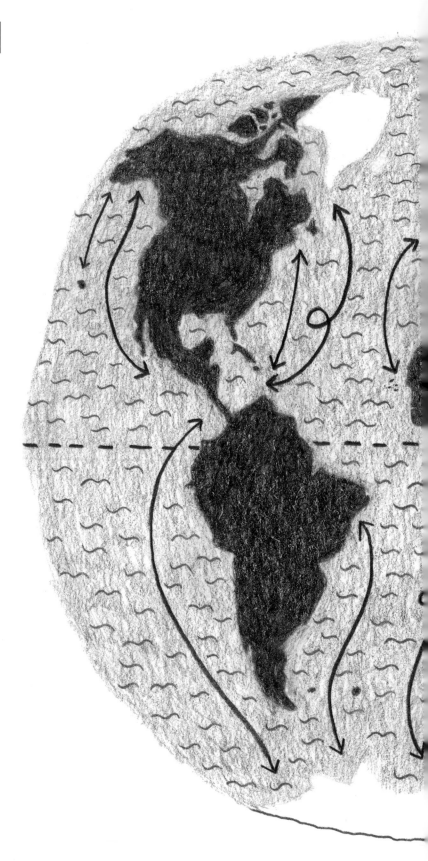

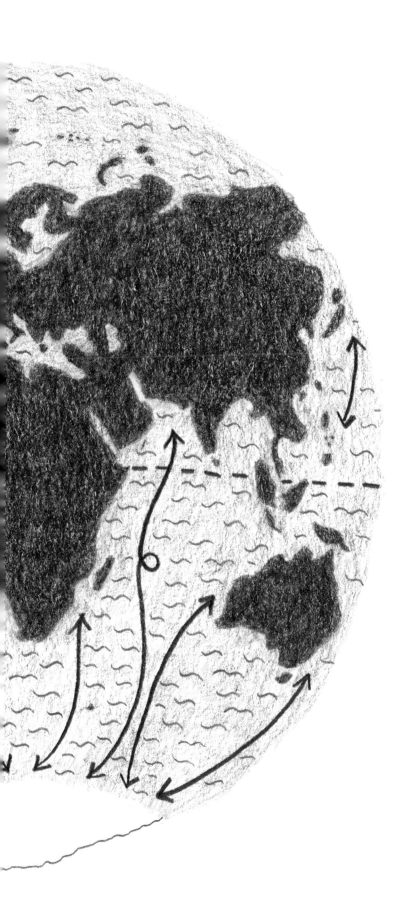

Among cetaceans, baleen whales are the biggest travelers. Among toothed whales, the sperm whale stands out: It travels extensively throughout the year.

Each species has its own favorite destination. For example, gray whales are famous for their voyages to lagoons on the Mexican coast each winter, before heading north in February to the cold waters around Alaska.

Here you can see some favorite routes of the humpback whale.

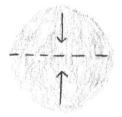

Migration to the **breeding** grounds (winter)

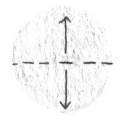

Migration to the **feeding** grounds (summer)

Alone or in Good Company

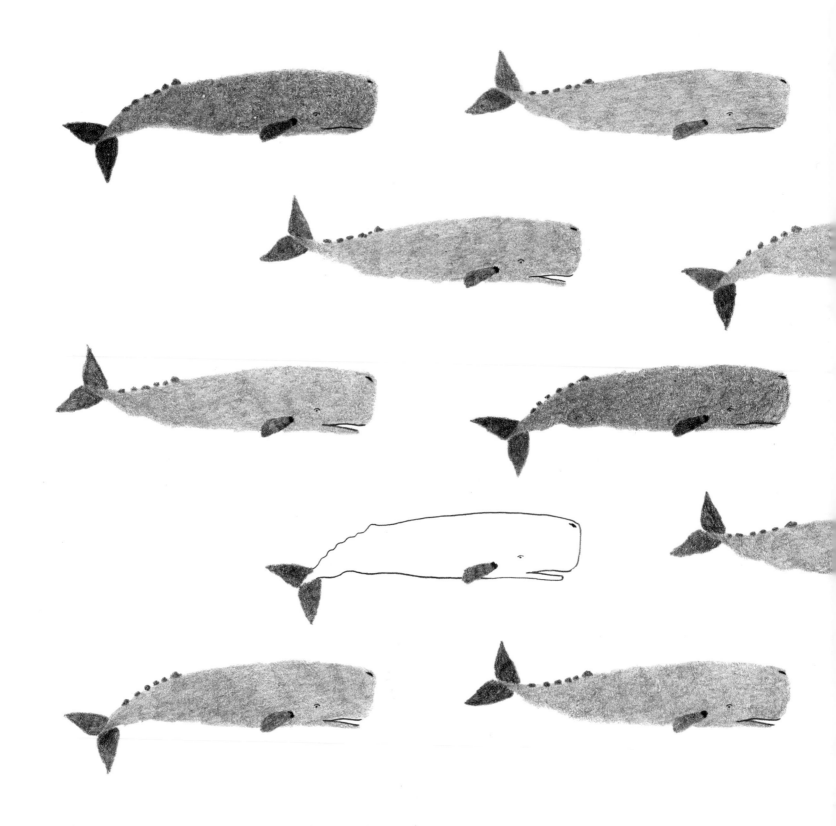

There is no limit to the number of whales that can live in a group, or **pod**.
For some species, whales can live alone, without any company, or travel in a group consisting of more than one hundred friends. There is a real social and hierarchical organization in these pods. They work together to get food and protect one another.

A special thing happens with humpback whales: When a baby is born, the mother will be accompanied by an **escort**.
Sperm whales definitely have the biggest pods—there can be as many as 150 members. Look below at a pod of sperm whales. If you look closely, you can see a white one, like the famous Moby-Dick.

Giants Since Childhood

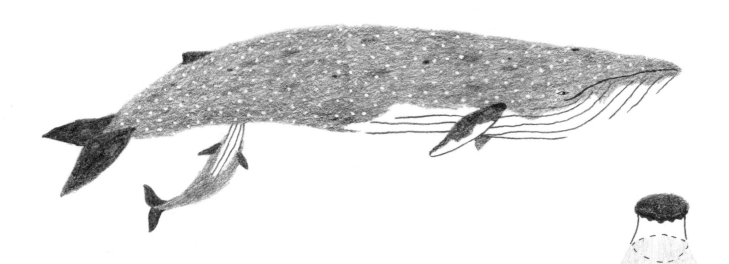

How Does a Whale's Life Begin?
Let's start from the beginning.
Pregnancy lasts about a year for most whales
except sperm whales, who have a gestation
period of eighteen months. The newborn is
already a giant. The pygmy right whale calf,
the smallest baleen of the bunch, is already
as long as an adult human. And this is
nothing compared to a blue whale calf, which
is 7 meters long at birth! The first thing a
newborn must do is breathe so, with the help
of its mother, it must get to the surface
immediately. The link between mother and calf
is especially close: In the best of cases, like the
Killer Whale, they remain together for life!

Milk, Milk, and More Milk
Some whale calves drink up to 400 liters
of milk per day. That's a bathtubful!
Nursing lasts about a year, but some
sperm whales, in spite of being grownups,
continue to drink their mother's milk
happily for around fifteen years!

Special Partnerships

Barnacles

Whales are so big that some animals confuse them for places to live.

This is precisely what happens with **barnacles**. Contrary to what many think, barnacles **are not parasites like whale lice**, who feed on sloughing skin.

Barnacles are only **guests** on the bodies of large cetaceans; they live on them but don't feed from them. These small animals are crustaceans.

They live inside pointed shells: because of this, they are also called *dogteeth*.

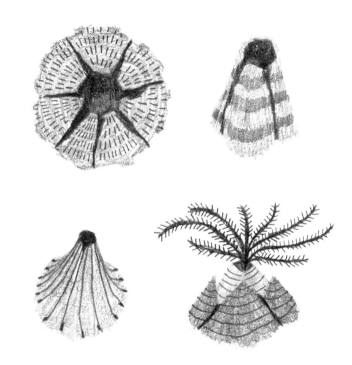

Remoras

Whereas barnacles see whales as somewhere to live, **remoras** instead think of them as a type of public transport.

These fish have a special part of their heads that can attach to surfaces like a **sucker**.

Remoras attach themselves to whales in order to travel quicker and, indirectly, receive protection from predators, who are awed by their big travel companions.

And Humans?

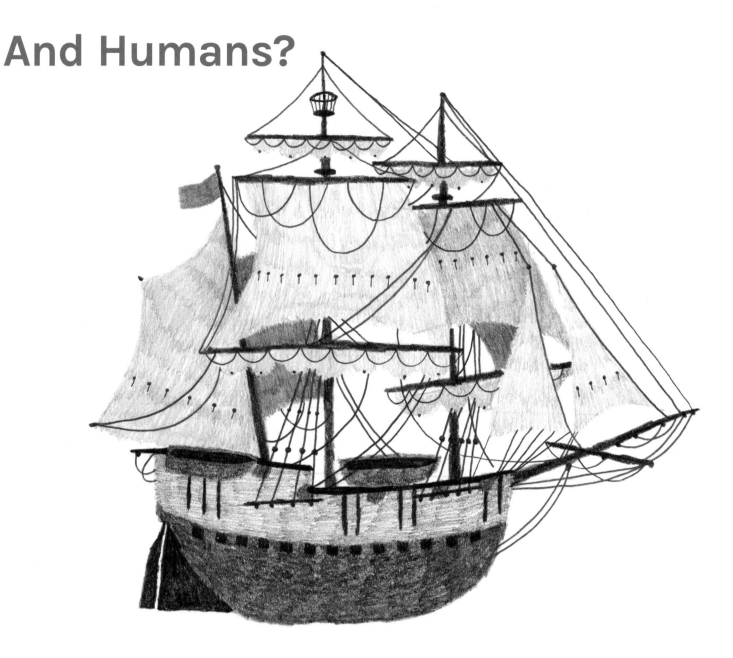

Hunting

Unfortunately, the relationship between whales and humans is mainly defined by **hunting**. Hunting has ancient origins. Nordic people were already hunting in 2000 BCE but whale hunting's most popular period was between 1700 and 1800 AD. Whale meat is not that tasty. Humans hunted them more for the **oil** that was extracted from the blubber, which was even known as liquid gold.

Sperm whale oil had a number of different uses, but it was mainly used to light lanterns in homes. Baleen whale oil was used more for cooking and cosmetics. In 1986, after critical decline of marine mammal populations, whale hunting was outlawed worldwide. Sadly, there are still some who try to get around those rules.

Captain Ahab is the most famous whale hunter in literature. In Herman Melville's novel *Moby-Dick*, Ahab's greatest obsession was the white sperm whale, Moby-Dick, that the captain never stopped chasing.

There are indigenous populations who continue to practice whaling using **traditional methods**.
As they live in some of the coldest parts of the world, whale hunting is necessary for their survival.

Whale Watching
Not everyone has bad intentions, however.
Whale watching means taking a trip to sea to meet these giant mammals and maybe even get a photograph of them.
You can go whale watching in many parts of the world.

One by One

Right Whale

Eubalaena australis (Southern Right Whale)
Eubalaena glacialis (Northern Right Whale)
Order: Cetacea
Suborder: Balaenidae
Family: Whale

Length: 36–59 ft (11–18 m)
Weight: 66,139–176,370 lb (30–80 T)

The right whale's skin
is mostly black.

They sometimes use
their **tail fins** like a ship's
sail to play.

The only visible white
spot is on the belly.

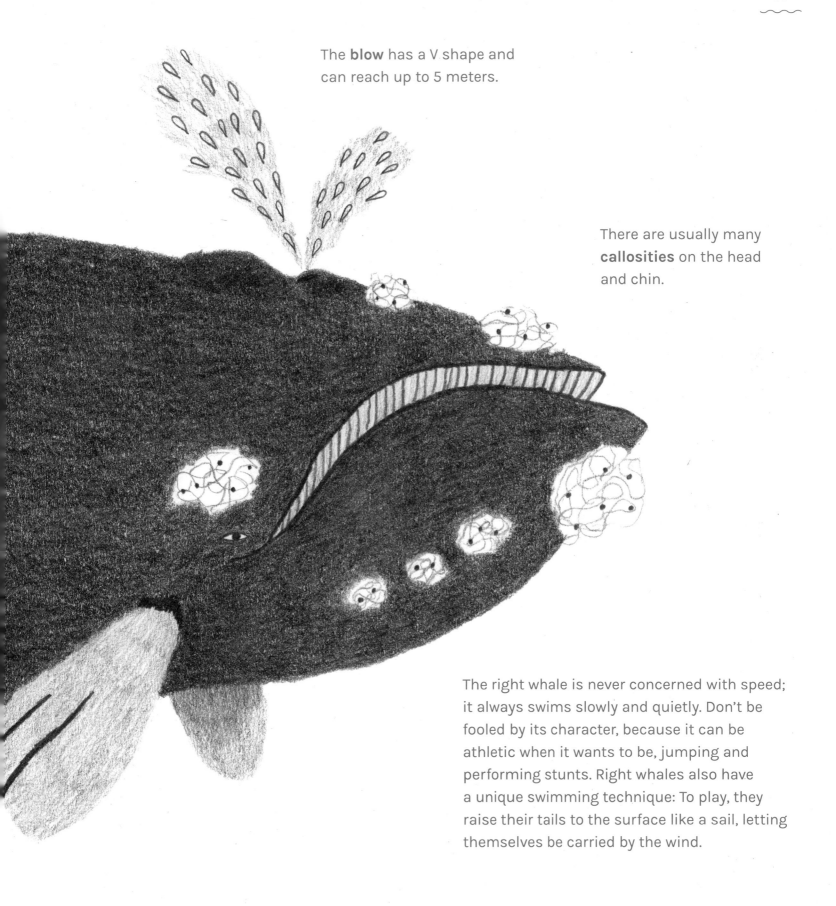

The **blow** has a V shape and can reach up to 5 meters.

There are usually many **callosities** on the head and chin.

The right whale is never concerned with speed; it always swims slowly and quietly. Don't be fooled by its character, because it can be athletic when it wants to be, jumping and performing stunts. Right whales also have a unique swimming technique: To play, they raise their tails to the surface like a sail, letting themselves be carried by the wind.

Bowhead Whale

Balaena mysticetus
Order: Cetacea
Suborder: Mysticeti
Family: Balaenidae

Length: 46–59 ft (14–18 m)
Weight: 132,277–220,462 lb (60–100 T)

Its color varies from black to bluish.

Some bowheads have a light spot near the **tail fin**.

Their **pectoral fins** have a shape similar to **paddles**.

Its **blow** is V-shaped and
rises up to 23 feet (7 m).

Its most characteristic
feature is a large white
patch under its chin.

Not much is known about the bowhead whale:
It is very shy and can't be seen easily. It loves
the cold and ice. It lives in the northern polar
regions near the layers of floating ice that
retreat and expand with changing temperatures.
In order to breathe, the bowhead whale
sometimes has to pierce a layer of ice to get
its head to the surface.

Pygmy Right Whale

Caperea marginata
Order: Cetacea
Suborder: Mysticeti
Family: Neobalaenidae

Length: 18–21 ft (5.5–6.5 m)
Weight: 6,614–7,716 lb (3–3.5 T)

It has a **dorsal fin** despite not being a rorqual.

Its belly is lighter in color than its back, which can vary from light gray to white.

It is difficult to recognize the pygmy right whale from its **blow,** as it is often small and indistinct.

Its **pectoral fins** are dark on the outside and light on the inside.

The pygmy right whale is the smallest of baleen whales. They are said to be rare, but they are probably just hiding from prying eyes. They are only shy with humans, though—you can sometimes see them swimming with other types of whales.

Gray Whale

Eschrichtius robustus
Order: Cetacea
Suborder: Mysticeti
Family: Eschrichtiidae

Length: 39–46 ft (12–14 m)
Weight: 33,069–77,162 lb (15–35 T)

It has a hump on its back,
which seems to be a hint
to a lost **dorsal fin**.

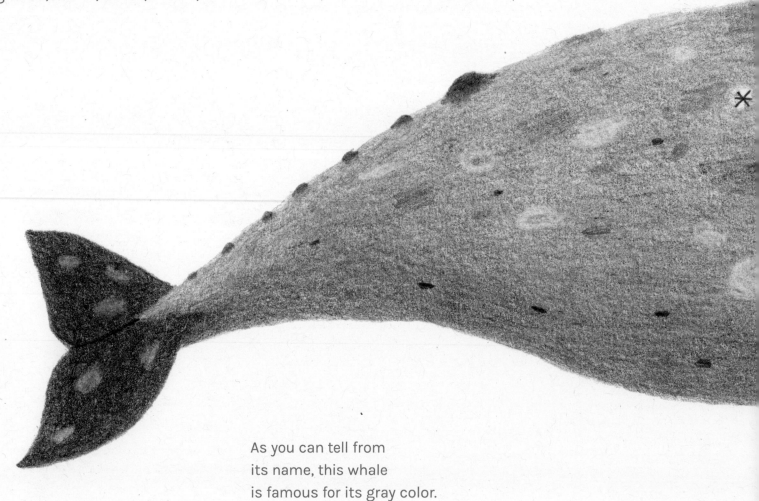

As you can tell from
its name, this whale
is famous for its gray color.

Its V-shaped **blow**
can reach up to
4 meters in height.

Its body can get infested
with **whale lice** and **barnacles**.

Gray whales are tireless travelers, more
so than any other mammal. They travel
the entire length of the North American coast
each year, from Alaska to Mexico. The whole
roundtrip is more than 12,427 miles (20,000 km)!
They are the only whales that feed on the
seabed, filtering the sand in search of small
crustaceans. They are also friendly towards
humans, letting us touch and stroke them
without shying away.

Humpback Whale

Megaptera novaeangliae
Order: Cetacea
Suborder: Mysticeti
Family: Balaen opteridae (rorqual)

Length: 38–49 ft (11.5–15 m)
Weight: 55,116–66,139 lb (25–30 T)

It has dark-colored skin, passing from blue and black to dark gray.

Their **pectoral fins** are their most characteristic feature: They are very long, reaching up to 16 feet (5 m). It is no coincidence that in Greek, the name *megaptere* means "large wings."

The black and white pigment under the **tail** is different for each whale, like our fingertips.

The **blow** is wider than it is tall, reaching up to 10 feet (3 m).

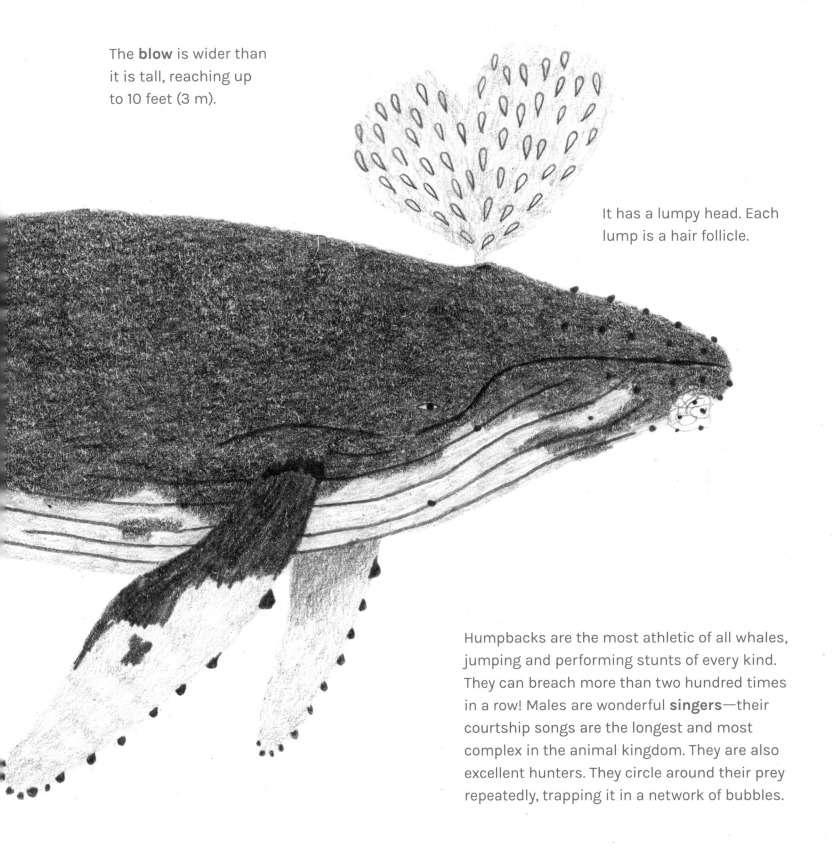

It has a lumpy head. Each lump is a hair follicle.

Humpbacks are the most athletic of all whales, jumping and performing stunts of every kind. They can breach more than two hundred times in a row! Males are wonderful **singers**—their courtship songs are the longest and most complex in the animal kingdom. They are also excellent hunters. They circle around their prey repeatedly, trapping it in a network of bubbles.

Blue Whale

Balaenoptera musculus
Order: Cetacea
Suborder: Mysticeti
Family: Balaenopteride (rorqual)

Length: 79–98 ft (24–30 m)
Weight: 264,555–396,832 lb (120–180 T)

The white spots extend over
the entire body.

Its name comes from
its characteristic
bluish-gray color.

The blue whale's **blow** can look like a geyser, reaching up to 30 feet (9 m) in height.

It has a light-colored belly with up to 90 ventral pleats (folds of skin).

The blue whale is the biggest animal on the planet, surpassing all others— including most extinct animals. To maintain its size, it needs to eat in abundance, devouring up to 8,818 pounds (4 T) of krill each day! But not everything heavy is slow. Despite its size, the blue whale is very fast, reaching speeds of up to 19 mph.

Fin Whale

Balaenoptera physalus
Order: Cetacea
Suborder: Mysticeti
Family: Balaenopteridae (rorqual)

Length: 59–72 ft (18–22 m)
Weight: 66,139–176,370 lb (30–80 T)

It has a very **dark back** and a light belly.

There are lighter patterns along its **back**.

Its **blow** consists of a single jet that reaches up to 20 feet (6 m).

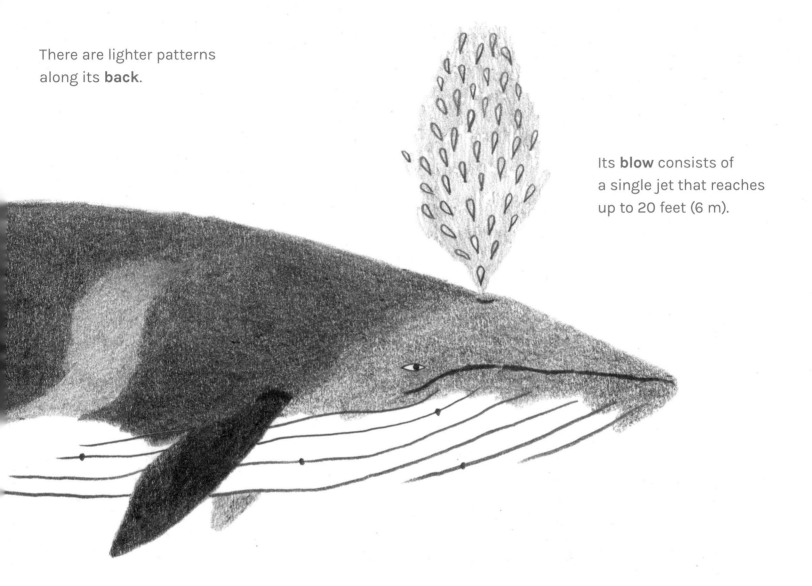

The coloring of its chin is **asymmetrical**: The right side is white, while the left side is dark, like the back.

The fin whale is the second largest animal in the world, after the blue whale. They look quite similar, and you can easily confuse one for the other, especially if seen in passing. This is one of the most common whales in waters north of the equator, and it can even be spotted in the Mediterranean Sea.

Minke Whale

Balaenoptera acutorostrata
Order: Cetacea
Suborder: Mysticeti
Family: Balaenopteridae (rorqual)

Length: 23–33 ft (7–10 m)
Weight: 11,023–33,069 lb (5–15 T)

Its **dorsal fin** is the most
developed of all rorquals.

The white coloring
of its belly can extend up
to the sides of its back.

Its **blow** rises up to
10 feet (3 m) in height,
but we rarely see it.

The color of its back varies
from black to brown.

The minke whale is the smallest whale
of its family. They are very curious creatures,
often spotted chasing boats. But if they
perceive danger, they can escape so quickly
that you wouldn't even realize that they had
gone! They often associate with seagulls as
fishing buddies, holding huge feasts together.

Its most distinctive
feature is a white patch
on its **pectoral fins**.

Sperm Whale

Physeter macrocephalus
Order: Cetacea
Suborder: Odontoceti
Family: Physeteridae

Length: 36–59 ft (11–18 m)
Weight: 44,093–110,231 lb (20–50 T)

It has a rounded hump
similar to a **dorsal fin**.

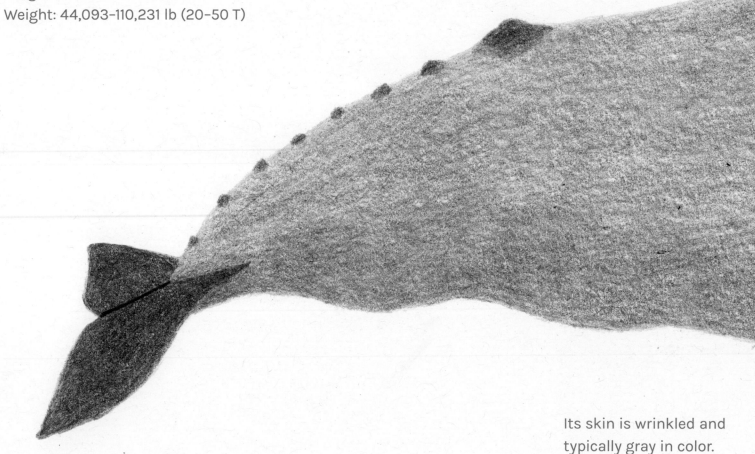

Its skin is wrinkled and
typically gray in color.

Its large **tail fin** has
a triangular shape.

Its **head** is enormous and usually covered with scars from fighting with giant squid, a major prey of the sperm whale.

It has a characteristic **blow** that is projected forward around 16 feet (5 m) in length and 7 feet (2 m) in height.

The most famous sperm whale is Moby-Dick, from Melville's novel of the same name. The sperm whale is the largest of all toothed whales. In fact, the sperm whale can be thought of as a dolphin because of its characteristics and tooth shape. Sperm whales are especially good at diving. They can reach 9,843 feet (3000 m) below sea level in search of squid, holding their breath for up to two hours.

Killer Whale

Orcinus orca
Order: Cetacea
Suborder: Odontoceti
Family: Delphinidae

Length: 18–33 ft (5.5–10 m)
Weight: 5,732–19,842 lbs (2.6–9 T)

It has unmistakable
coloring: completely black,
except for a white belly and
spot above the eye. It also has
a characteristic saddle patch
behind the dorsal fin that is used
to identify individual whales.

The killer whale's **caudal fin**,
or fluke, is black on one side
and white on the other.

The **dorsal fin** is particularly developed in males: it can be up to 7 feet (2 m) tall.

The **blow** is especially visible when in contact with cold air.

The shape of its large **pectoral fins** is similar to that of a spade.

Killer whales have particularly close **family units**, remaining together for a lifetime. And each pod "speaks" its own special **dialect**! Don't let their reputation as ferocious beasts fool you—killer whales don't attack humans. They are actually quite curious and sometimes even approach us.

Select Bibliography

Carrada, Giovanni. *Communicating Science: A Survival Kit for Researchers*. Milan, Italy: Sironi, 2005.

Carwardine, Mark. *Whales, Dolphins, and Porpoises*. New York: DK, 2002.

Carwardine, Mark, R. Ewan Fordyce, Peter Gill, and Erich Hoyt. *Whales, Dolphins, and Porpoises*. New York: HarperCollins, 1998.

Henriques, Ricardo. Ocean: *A Visual Miscellany*. Lisbon, Portugal: Pato Logico, 2012.

"Kingdom of the Blue Whale Blue Whale Facts." National Geographic Channel, channel.nationalgeographic.com/channel/content/kingdom-of-the-blue-whale-3302/blue-whale-facts.

Russell, Harriet. *Drawing in the Sea*. Mantua, Italy: Corraini, 2013.

Scammon, Charles Melville. *The Marine Mammals of the North-Western Coast of North America, Described and Illustrated, Together with an Account of the American Whale-Fishery*. San Francisco: J. H. Carmany, 1874.

Stamback, Shawn. "Whales Almost Eat Divers (Original Version)." July 20, 2013. YouTube Video, 1:16. youtube.com/watch?v=0Ut7wK9l9mk.

Wurtz, Maurizio and Nadia Repetto. *Dolphins and Whales*. Translated by Studio Traduzioni, Vecchia Milan. Vercelli, Italy: White Star, 2003.

Some Places to Watch Whales

ANTARCTIC PENINSULA
Minke, humpback, and orca whales (*February and March*)

AUSTRALIA
Hervey Bay
Grown humpback whales (*mid-July to the end of October*)

CANADA
Canadian Arctic
Beluga, narwhal, and bowhead whales (*June to August*)

Nunavut
Beluga whales (*July to early August*); narwhal whales (*June*)

Vancouver Island
Orca whales (*mid-June to October*)

DOMINICA, CARIBBEAN
Sperm whales (*November to April*)

ICELAND
Minke, humpback, blue, and orca whales (*May to September; blue whales mainly June to early July*)

MEXICO
Baja California
Humpback, sperm, minke, and gray whales (*February to April*)

NEW ZEALAND
Kaikoura
Sperm whales (*year-round*)

SCOTLAND
Isle of Mull
Minke, humpback, fin, sperm, pilot, and orca whales (*May to September*)

SOUTH AFRICA
Hermanus
Southern right whales (*May to November*)

Western Cape
Southern right and humpback whales (*June to November; peak is October*)

UNITED STATES
Alaska
Glacier Bay
Humpback, minke, orca, and blue whales (*June to August*)

Juneau
Humpback and orca whales (*April to November*)

California
Big Sur
Gray and humpback whales (*year-round*)
Monterey Bay
Humpback, blue, and gray whales (*year-round*)
San Diego
Gray, blue, and fin whales (*mid-December to mid-March; mid-June to September*)

Florida (Jacksonville)
North Atlantic right whales (*November to April*)

Hawaii (Maui)
Humpback whales (*December to April*)

Massachusetts (Cape Cod)
Minke, fin, and humpback whales (*April to October*)

Maine (Bar Harbor)
Fin, minke, and right whales (*mid-April to October*)

New York (Long Island)
Fin, humpback, minke, sperm, North Atlantic right, and blue whales (*July to early September*)

Oregon (Depoe Bay)
Gray Whales (*mid-December to June*)

Virginia (Virginia Beach)
Humpback whales (*December to March*)

Washington (San Juan Islands)
Orca whales (*April to September*)

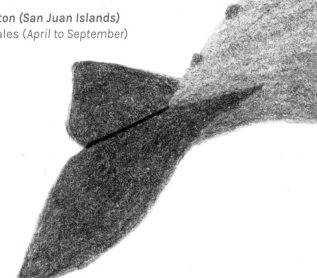

Index

NOTE: Page numbers in *italics* refer to illustrations.